# NECESSARY
# TARGETS

# NECESSARY TARGETS

## A Story of Women and War

### EVE ENSLER

VILLARD

NEW YORK

Published in the United States by Villard Books, an
imprint of The Random House Publishing Group, a division of
Random House, Inc., New York, and simultaneously in Canada
by Random House of Canada Limited, Toronto.

VILLARD BOOKS and "V" CIRCLED Design are registered
trademarks of Random House, Inc.

Library of Congress Cataloging-in-Publication Data
Ensler, Eve.
Necessary targets: a story of women and war [a play] / Eve Ensler.
　　　p.　　cm.
ISBN 978-0-375-75603-0
1. Women refugees—Drama.　2. Americans—Bosnia and
Hercegovina—Drama.
3. Bosnia and Hercegovina—Drama.　I. Title.
PS3555.N75 N43　　2000
812'.54—dc21　　　00-038223

www.villard.com

Printed in the United States of America

6 8 9 7

Book design by Caroline Cunningham

For Rada Boric and the women of Bosnia,
and, of course, for you, Ariel

# CONTENTS

# INTRODUCTION

We make decisions all the time. Decisions about them. Them is always different from us. Them has no face. Them is a little bit deserving of all the bad that happens to them. Them is used to violence—it's in their blood.

There are rules about them. We keep them over there, out of sight, conceptual. We do not get close enough to touch or smell or know them. We do not want to see how easily we could become them—how quickly violence arrives, how swiftly people turn, embracing racist hate. We do not want to know or touch the parts of ourselves that are capable of behaving like them.

Sometimes, if we are lucky, an image, a poem, an invitation to a foreign place pierces our perception. We suddenly stare down at a photograph on the cover of *Newsday*—six young Bosnian girls just returned from a rape camp. Their faces are beautiful and young and destroyed. We see their utter incomprehension and terror. We feel their shame.

We are compelled. We go and meet them—young, old, Muslim, Croatian, Serbian, Haitian, Rwandan, Afghan, Chechen. We sit in dusty barracks, makeshift refugee camps, peeling centers. We hold the strong, earthbound hands of the farmers longing for their land, we walk through beet fields with the woman with strawberry stains as she describes the execution of her parents, we sit in a hot room in a crowded refugee hotel with a mother and six children and one son who lies suspended in a bed, mute from three months in a concentration camp. We watch woman after woman shake, pace, smoke, choke, weep as they describe the gang rapes, the public rapes, the rapes of mothers, sisters, and grandmothers. We see how they have lost their homes and identities. That they do not eat or can't stop eating. We hear how they did not expect this or want this and our secure usness, our little usness, begins to unravel. It is dangerous.

In 1993, I went to the former Yugoslavia to interview Bosnian women war refugees. For my first ten days in Zagreb, I slept on a couch in the Center for Women War Victims. The center was created to serve

Muslim, Croatian, and Serbian women refugees who had been raped and made homeless by war. Most of the women who worked there were refugees themselves. They ran support groups and provided emergency aid, food, toiletries, medication, children's toys. They helped women find employment, access to medical treatment, and schools for their children.

When we think of war, we think of it as something that happens to men in fields or jungles. We think of hand grenades and Scud missiles. We think of the moment of violence—the blast, the explosion. But war is also a consequence—the effects of which are not known or felt for months, years, generations. And because consequences are usually not televised, by then the war is no longer sexy—the ratings are gone, consequences remain invisible. It is the bombing, the explosions in the dark, that keep us watching. As long as there are snipers outside of Sarajevo, Sarajevo exists. But after the bombing, after the snipers, that's when the real war begins.

It is found in the broken-down fabric of community, in the death of trust, in the destruction of the everyday patterns of living. It is found in trauma and depression, poverty and homelessness and starvation. It is found in the emasculation and rage of the victim, in the new violence; the traumatized soldier beating his wife, the teenage boys already plotting revenge, the ongoing panic of the children.

When we think of war, we do not think of women. Because the work of survival, of restoration, is not glamorous work. Like most women's work, it is undervalued, underpaid, and impossible. After war, men are often shattered, unable to function. Women not only work, but they create peace networks, find ways to bring about healing. They teach in home schools when the school buildings are destroyed. They build gardens in the middle of abandoned railroad tracks. They pick up the pieces, although they usually haven't fired a gun.

*Necessary Targets* is based on the stories of the women I met and heard in Bosnia. It was their community, their holding on to love, their insane humanity in the face of catastrophe, their staggering refusal to have or seek revenge that fueled me and ultimately moved me to write this play.

After my first week on the Center for Women War Victims couch, where I'd been interviewing women eight to twelve hours a day, a woman activist, Rachel, offered me her apartment for the weekend. I was both relieved and terrified to have a moment to stop, to actually absorb all the trauma and terror of the stories I had heard. As I lay in Rachel's bed, trying to avoid the terrible images in my head, avoiding the trajectory of my heart, which was heavy and downward-moving, I realized I was not sleeping. I was not moving or thinking. I was suspended.

Although I did not feel grace or the presence of anything remotely resembling God, I sensed this suspension was a kind of involuntary prayer, a call to make Bosnia matter. To make war matter. But how do you make destruction matter? How do you make people's suffering thousands of miles away matter? How do you make this world, this life, in all its mystery and injustice, matter?

Maybe this is the purpose of art, and theater in particular—to experience what we experience, to see what's in front of us, to allow the truth in, with all its sorrow and brutality, because in the theater we are not alone in our worried and stained beds. We are there, for these moments together, joined by what we see and hear, made stronger, hopefully, by what opens us.

# NECESSARY
# TARGETS

# SCENE 1

*Lights up on a posh living room. A coffee table with plates of food.* J.S., *a stunning, reserved woman near fifty, sits with* MELISSA, *a young, strong woman who sits awkwardly on the sofa, drinking water.* MELISSA *wipes up the excess water that her drink has left on the coffee table.* J.S. *moves a round wooden object toward her.*

### MELISSA

Oh, it's a coaster. I thought it was an art object. I'm so sorry.

### J.S.

Not to worry. It's an old table.

### MELISSA

It's gorgeous. In such amazing shape. There's not one

smudge on it. I could never keep a table like that. It
takes so much time.

                          J.S.

Well, I don't spend my days polishing the table.


                        MELISSA

No, no. I'm sure you have someone who does that.
      *(They both laugh nervously.)*

                          J.S.

You're younger than I expected.


                        MELISSA

Well, I've been through a lot.


                          J.S.

      *(unconsciously therapeutic)*
Yes?


                        MELISSA

      *(sensing she's being analyzed, suddenly)*
Oh, I didn't mean it like that.


                          J.S.

Like what?

MELISSA

Like that. Like childhood. Like poor me. I don't feel sorry for myself.

J.S.

Why would I think that?

MELISSA

Because you're a shrink. Because I'm sure you'll attribute all I do now to all that happened to me when I was little.

J.S.

I don't know what happened to you when you were little, Melissa.

MELISSA

Do you need to know? Is it important for you to know? I'd rather not be identified or determined by that part of my life. It was their life. This is my life.

J.S.

And what makes this *your* life?

MELISSA

That feels very much like a shrink question.

Oh, I'm sorry.

> *(They sit awkwardly.)*

J.S.

I like your shoes.

MELISSA

You do?

J.S.

Yes, very much.

MELISSA

Kenneth Cole. I love the zippers.

J.S.

They're very . . . definitive.

MELISSA

Well . . . yes. They're grounding. I need shoes that are grounding.

J.S.

Yes. I imagine.

MELISSA

Not 'cause I'm crazy or off-the-wall or anything. But these situations, these wars. One needs . . . grounding.

J.S.

Yes. Your résumé's impressive. You come highly recommended.

MELISSA

Oh, I just made it up for you. I mean, typed it . . . up for you. All the facts are true. I usually work alone. I don't have to prove myself. So this is new.

J.S.

It's really interesting. You're trained as a therapist and a writer. That's very unusual.

MELISSA

Trauma counselor.

J.S.

What?

MELISSA

I'm trained as a trauma counselor. It's very specific

training. I am not a therapist. I only work with seriously traumatized populations. Oh God, listen to me,
"seriously traumatized populations . . ."

Doesn't it frighten you?

MELISSA

Yes, definitely. But it scares me more not to see it, not
to know what's going on. Why are you going to Bosnia?

J.S.

I am going for the President's commission. I was asked,
and it's a huge honor. To be honest, I was a bit surprised. I mean, Bosnia is not a place I know very much
about. I read the news, but until about a week ago, the
Balkans were not exactly next on my vacation map.

MELISSA

Why does this commission want you to be there?

J.S.

Well, they chose a range of professions for the team.
I'm the "shrink" piece, as you say. At one time it was
my field, trauma.

MELISSA

Yes, eating disorders. I am familiar with your books.

J.S.

Yes?

MELISSA

You have never been to a war-torn country.

J.S.

God, no. That's why I wanted you to be with me, Melissa. Your experience.

MELISSA

War is not exactly the same as anorexia.

J.S.

I am a psychiatrist. Twenty-six years. In private practice. I've been involved in a war of sorts, mental skirmishes and attacks. Trauma is trauma.

MELISSA

In Haiti, the psychiatrists were fleeing like flies.

J.S.

Haiti?

MELISSA

Yes.

J.S.

How long were you there?

MELISSA

Eight months.

J.S.

Weren't you afraid?

MELISSA

No. Not in Haiti—in Rwanda, yes . . .

J.S.

Rwanda.

MELISSA

Yes.

J.S.

I can't imagine.

MELISSA

No. No one could imagine.

J.S.

Are you sure you're ready to go to Bosnia, to do this
again?

MELISSA

(clipped)

It's my work. It's what I do.

J.S.

You are very strong. So young and so strong.

MELISSA

Is this commission the real deal? Or is it one of those
U.N. situations—observe/witness, but do not go near?

J.S.

They said we would be working directly with the
women war refugees. It's very "hands-on." That's why I
need you to be my assistant.

MELISSA

Is that what you were told?

J.S.

What?

MELISSA

That I was an assistant—that I'd be your assistant.

J.S.

Yes, you were to assist me. You are a war specialist and you were to assist me.

MELISSA

I am currently writing a book—investigating the effect of war in the creation and development of trauma, focusing primarily on communities of women, on those specific atrocities that traumatize women. It's my first contract with a major publisher. It's actually your publisher. It is essential that I complete the book this year. I will need to interview these women.

J.S.

That shouldn't be a problem.
(J.S. *offers her a plate of food.*)

J.S.

Don't you want something, Melissa? There are some lovely chicken-pesto wraps.

MELISSA

It's hard to eat on an interview. The crumbs. The chewing. Besides, I don't eat meat.

J.S.

Oh, you're a vegetarian.

MELISSA

Yes.

J.S.

That must be difficult when you travel. Isn't it hard to find something to eat?

MELISSA

I eat okay. I eat!

J.S.

Is there something else I can get you—fruit, nuts?

MELISSA

No, I'm fine.
*(They sit awkwardly.)*

What does one wear?

MELISSA

Where?

J.S.

In a war-torn country.

MELISSA

You'll need a bulletproof vest, flak jacket, mud-stomping boots.

J.S.

(unnerved)
Really?

MELISSA

Yes, and a helmet.

J.S.

Really?

MELISSA

No, we're not going as soldiers.

What are we going *as*?

MELISSA

Well, you're going as an appointee of the President, and
I, well, I guess I'm going as your assistant.
*(MELISSA suddenly spills her drink. She frantically tries
to wipe it up.)*

J.S.

Don't worry, Melissa. It's only water.

MELISSA

But it's on this table . . .

J.S.

I make you nervous.

MELISSA

Like I said, it's what I can't see that frightens me.
*(They stare awkwardly at one another, oddly frozen.)*

# SCENE 2

*Bosnia. A refugee camp. A barracks-like room. Desolate. Two cots. Emptiness—a feeling of poverty.* MELISSA *is making her bed, unpacking.* J.S. *enters, dressed in her proper New York City clothes.*

J.S.

There are big, dirty footprints in the bathroom.

MELISSA

Yes, you squat in them.

J.S.

You mean to . . .

MELISSA

(laughs at her)

Poop. Yes, you squat to poop.

J.S.

In the footprints.

MELISSA

Yes. It's actually better . . .

J.S.

For . . . ?

MELISSA

Your colon.

J.S.

And the showers.

MELISSA

They're pretty foul, but you'll get used to them.

J.S.

They were used for cattle.

MELISSA

Clean cattle.

J.S.

The hotel would give us some distance.

MELISSA

That's the problem with it. The women will resent us living in such luxury.

J.S.

But I am not a refugee.

MELISSA

It will bring us closer to them.

J.S.

I think it's insulting. To pretend to be living in these conditions. They know we can leave.

MELISSA

You can go.

J.S.

You'll excuse me, but I need the little comforts. You're

younger than I. I welcome a bath, clean sheets, and a place to sit to . . .

MELISSA

Poop. These women need those same comforts. They had them all before the war.

J.S.

I don't think squatting in filthy footprints will make me a more effective therapist. Frankly, I think it will irritate me. I will be less patient and cranky.

MELISSA

Well, we don't want you cranky.

(They both laugh.)

MELISSA

Listen, I can help find you a hotel.

(J.S. turns to leave, then turns back. She reluctantly throws her suitcase on the bed. She begins to unpack. MELISSA stares into her suitcase.)

MELISSA

God, who packed your bags? Bendel's?

I can't help it. I'm organized.


MELISSA

Organized? Even your socks are wrapped in tissue paper!

> (MELISSA *moves closer to examine. She picks up the socks.*)


MELISSA

What kind of socks are they?

> (J.S. *grabs her socks back and moves* MELISSA *away from her bag.*)


J.S.

Do you have an issue with comfort?


MELISSA

Is that a shrink question?


J.S.

No, it was actually an innocent question.


MELISSA

Is that possible?

Melissa, believe it or not, sometimes I'm just curious about you, as a person. We are traveling together. It's a human thing.

MELISSA

*(pause)* Actually, I'm not big on comfort. It tends to terrorize me.

J.S.

I won't even go there.

# SCENE 3

*Barracks room—empty, broken-down. Torn cotton cloths on the window. Very hot. Six chairs in a semicircle, a tray of coffee on the table, little Turkish coffee cups.* JELENA, *an earthy woman in her late forties;* ZLATA, *a distinguished and sophisticated woman the same age as* J.S.; NUNA, *a very Americanized teenager;* SEADA, *a beautiful girl in her twenties;* AZRA, *an oldie from the village.* J.S. *and* MELISSA *sit in the chairs. Most of the women are smoking, staring at* J.S., *taking in her clothes, etc. After a long time,* J.S. *finally speaks.*

J.S.

Hello.

WOMEN

Hello.

#### J.S.

I'm Dr. . . . J.S. And this is my assistant, Melissa.

*(uncomfortable, but full of therapist façade)*

As most of you already know, we have been brought here by the presidential commission. Although Melissa has a great deal of experience in conflict zones, I must admit that war is new to me.

#### JELENA

Join the club.

*(The women laugh.)*

#### J.S.

So I will be learning with you as we go along.

#### AZRA

So you're a loony doctor.

#### JELENA

No, she is a doctor for crazy people.

#### AZRA

Are we crazy?

#### NUNA

Yes, she heard how you kicked your dog.

#### AZRA

I did not kick Tessa. I love Tessa more than I love most of you.

#### J.S.

We thought we'd start off with group sessions in the morning and afternoon. Two hours per session. We'd like to begin and end on time. So we'd appreciate your cooperation.

#### AZRA

I did not kick Tessa. I love my animals. I had a cow, oh what a cow! She could make enough milk . . .

#### EVERYONE

*(all the Bosnian women)*

. . . to feed a village.

#### MELISSA

We will also be available to you when we are not in session. As you know, we are staying here in the camp for that purpose. *(looks at* J.S.*)* So don't hesitate to call on us. Anytime.

> *(*J.S. *has to put her glasses on in order to read* NUNA*'s name tag.)*

J.S.

No-ni. *(mispronounces it, and the women correct her; embarrassed, she begins again)* Nuni. *(the women correct her again; she very nervously tries again)* Nuna, why don't you begin?

NUNA

Begin what?

J.S.

Wherever you are. Start right there.

NUNA

You mean talk.

J.S.

If that's what you'd like to do.

NUNA

Why did you pick me? Do I look sicker than the others?
> *(The women laugh.)*

J.S.

Is that how you feel?

NUNA

I didn't before.

J.S.

Before what?

NUNA

Before you picked me. Before you made me talk. Is it because I'm young? Do I look particularly disturbed? I don't do drugs.

J.S.

Do you normally go through this much when you are asked to speak?

NUNA

There is nothing normal here. Not for a long time.

J.S.

What was normal like for you?

NUNA

What is normal like for anyone? What is normal like
for you? You know normal.

J.S.

I'd love for you to tell me about it, Nuna.

NUNA

I don't know. You are asking me so many things. Is this
therapy? In America everyone's in therapy, right?

MELISSA

*(laughing)*
Well, not everyone.

NUNA

I have heard that the patient—that's what we're
called—lies down and goes into a trance and has visions
and then they get to be rich.

J.S.

*(stepping in to help)*
Are you from Bosnia, Nuna?

#### MELISSA

Of course she's from Bosnia.

#### ZLATA

We're all from Bosnia. What do you think we're doing here?

#### J.S.

*(to ZLATA)*
What is your name?

#### JELENA

My name is Jelena. We are very honored that you Americans came all the way here. This is Azra. Azra's from Banja Luka.

#### AZRA

I need a doctor.

#### ZLATA

She is not that kind of doctor.

#### AZRA

I'm sure she knows something about arthritis. All doctors know about arthritis.

ZLATA

She's not that kind of doctor. I've already looked at you. It's simply old age.

JELENA

This is Seada, the gorgeous one. She is from the country. She never went outside her village before the war. And this is our Zlata, a doctor. You will have a hard time winning Zlata. You've already met Nuna. Nuna has seen too many American movies. Oh yes . . . and, of course, Doona . . .

(SEADA *holds out a wrapped little baby.*)

SEADA

(*to* J.S.)
You are so pretty and so modern.

ZLATA

(*slightly sarcastic*)
There was a war going on in Bosnia. We are refugees.

AZRA

Why don't you get those leaders on the couches? They're the loony ones.

### SEADA

Doona is laughing. She is happy you are here.

### MELISSA

How old is Doona?

(SEADA *holds out her wrapped baby and giggles.*)

### ZLATA

What do you want with us?

### J.S.

I have come here . . . well *(looking at Melissa)*, we have come here . . . to help you.

*(Everyone stares at her.)*

### ZLATA

And how do you plan to do that?

### J.S.

I . . . well . . . we . . . I am a clinical therapist and you have . . .

### AZRA

Will you get me my goats and cow? Will you get my salami? They took my salami.

#### JELENA

They are not here for that, Azra.

#### MELISSA

We are here to help you, well . . . talk.

#### ZLATA

There is no shortage of talking here.

#### NUNA

All we do is talk and talk . . .

#### ZLATA

We are sick of talking.

#### J.S.

We are here to help you talk about the war, about the . . .

*(The women laugh.)*

#### ZLATA

You flew all the way here for that? Two American doctors to "help" a group of poor Bosnian refugees talk about the war? What did you think we were talking about before you came? Our lingerie, our dinner parties . . .

NUNA

No, our face-lifts . . .

(The women laugh again.)

MELISSA

We are very moved by what you've been through. We were hoping you would talk to us. You would tell us your stories.

ZLATA

You and everybody else. They came from everywhere at the beginning of the war to hear the gory details.

NUNA

We read about ourselves in the paper. They made us sound deranged.

JELENA

And the scarf, always the scarf. Pictures of Azra with the scarf.

NUNA

They never took pictures of me.

ZLATA

They left and they never came back.

MELISSA

Exactly. That's why I'm writing a book, not an article. It is important that people know your stories the way you want to tell them.

ZLATA

So you are doctors or journalists?

J.S.

We are therapists. Well . . . Melissa is . . .

MELISSA

(overlapping)

I am working on a book composed of the stories of refugees all around the world.

ZLATA

Oh, so we're a chapter.

MELISSA

No, no . . .

ZLATA

And who do you think will read your book?

MELISSA

I am hoping it will be read everywhere. Would anyone object to my recording our sessions?

ZLATA

I would not like you to record anything I say. I would not like that.

MELISSA

We will . . .

J.S.

. . . not record you, Zlata. Are there others who feel this way?

MELISSA

I know it's difficult, but you will be helping so many people—to know your stories, to get them out.

J.S.

And you do not have to be so generous. You have already been through so much.

ZLATA

We had bad experiences with journalists.

J.S.

We are not journalists.

MELISSA

My writing is not to exploit you. Traumatized war victims . . .

NUNA

Is that what we're called? Traumatized war victims? Sounds so spooky.

MELISSA

It's not a judgment.

JELENA

No, worse, it's a life sentence. We are not wanted anywhere because we stink.

SEADA

Doona smells so pretty. She smells like doves.

ZLATA

I do not want you recording me.

J.S.

Nothing is being taped today.

**NUNA**

So this is American therapy?

**AZRA**

It just feels like another terrible day to me.

# SCENE 4

*Barracks room with two cots.* J.S. *is furiously packing when* MELISSA *enters.*

MELISSA

What are you doing?

J.S.

Packing. I'm going home. This is ridiculous. Coming to Bosnia to help refugees talk about the war.

MELISSA

I thought you were a trained psychiatrist. Trained to see through denial and well-constructed defenses.

J.S.

That has nothing to do with this.

MELISSA

This is normal, what you're going through.

J.S.

I am totally embarrassed. I feel ludicrous.

MELISSA

And when a patient who's been badly abused comes to
you, do you panic, do you give up if you don't have life
experiences to compare?

J.S.

Listen. I can't help these women. They need homes, a
country, and care.

MELISSA

It's only the first day. We're stirring things up. It means
the transference is working.

J.S.

I do not sense transference. I sense their rightful con-
tempt at being patronized.

MELISSA

I thought you were stronger than this.

My practice is very limited. I like it that way.

MELISSA

These women need an outlet for their rage and despair.
We are necessary targets.

(J.S. *looks at* MELISSA.)

MELISSA

I've been in other wars. It always begins like this.

J.S.

How does it end?

MELISSA

They tell their stories.

J.S.

Yes, but they don't get to go home?

(NUNA *comes running in.*)

NUNA

We need you to come. Baby Doona won't stop crying.
Seada's worried that Doona's choking, and I'm worried

the women are going to choke Seada if Doona doesn't
shut up.

(MELISSA *runs out.* NUNA *stops and looks at* J.S., *who
doesn't move.*)

#### NUNA

Aren't you coming? We're really very friendly once you
get to know us. And you should know, we've already
talked and agreed. We think you're a little nervous, but
we love the way you dress. You remind us of Meryl
Streep.

(MELISSA *enters, carrying* DOONA.)

#### J.S.

How's the baby?

#### MELISSA

She's gonna talk, she's gonna tell us what happened.

(J.S. *looks out.*)

# SCENE 5

*AZRA and JELENA sit at a table drinking little shots of alcohol.*
*J.S. listens in the shadows, unseen by them.*

### JELENA

Dado. My Dado.

### AZRA

What?

### JELENA

Dado. Dado. He was so young then and handsome and
eager. He was so eager to climb between the sheets, any
time of day or night, and he was good there. So tender
and . . .

AZRA

*(cutting her off)*

Please, Jelena. Please. Give me my cows. Cows are friendly. Cows are simple. My cow . . .

JELENA

Dado loved me, Azra. His late-day face returning from the fields. Always he thought to bring me a vegetable, a ripe tomato, a luscious cucumber, or a flower. Always for me. Always for me.

AZRA

My goats ate all the flowers. I didn't mind. Well, I did, but I don't now. Oh what I would give to see my goats eat the flowers.

JELENA

Dado's so tired now.

AZRA

We're all tired now.

JELENA

It's different with Dado. He's changed. He's so angry

all the time. He won't touch me except to . . . he won't talk to me.

AZRA

Cows. Goats. They always talk. They always listen.

JELENA

But sex, Azra, you need a man for sex.

AZRA

Yuck . . .

JELENA

Have you never had sex, Azra?

AZRA

Yuck . . .

JELENA

Oh, come on. There must have been someone, once. A kiss? A quick feel in the barn?

AZRA

Cows. Only cows.

You would like sex. When we get home, I will get you a
man. Believe me, it's better than salami.

*(Lights fade on* AZRA *and* JELENA, *and* J.S. *watching and
listening in the shadows.)*

# SCENE 6

*Dark. Nighttime in the barracks.* J.S. *and* MELISSA *are asleep. Suddenly a dark shadow appears and grabs* J.S. *She sits up and screams. The shadow figure screams back and we then see that it's* SEADA *with her baby,* DOONA, *in her arms.* J.S. *tries to gain her composure.* MELISSA *watches their interaction from her bed, saying nothing.*

J.S.

I'm sorry, Seada. I didn't mean to frighten you.

SEADA

*(climbing into* J.S.*'s bed)*

Oh, Mama, let me in quickly, please. It's cold in my room. It's so much warmer in your bed.

*(*J.S. *becomes extremely uncomfortable.* J.S. *sits up, preventing* SEADA *from getting into the bed.)*

J.S.

You miss your mother, Seada.

SEADA

*(continuing her need to get into the bed)*
Hold me, Mama.

J.S.

You're a little lost, Seada. I think if you could talk about your feelings, we may be able to help you find out where you are.

SEADA

I'm tired, Mama. I don't want to talk. I want to sleep . . . with you.

J.S.

*(becoming very uptight)*
It's not appropriate, Seada.

SEADA

I don't know what that means.

J.S.

It would not help you. It's important you have boundaries. They are essential to help you heal.

#### SEADA

*(begins to cry)*

Doona is freezing, Mama. If we could just lie close like
we always do. If we could just lie close, Mama.

*(SEADA defiantly and gently gets into bed. J.S. is stiff,
trying to remain professional. SEADA wraps herself
around her. J.S. pats her in an awkward, embarrassed
kind of way.)*

#### SEADA

Would you sing to me, Mama?

#### J.S.

It's late now, Seada. I think it's best you just sleep.

#### SEADA

Are you afraid, Mama? Are you afraid too?

*(SEADA pats J.S. on her head to comfort her and then
puts her head on J.S.'s very tense breast. J.S. looks over at
MELISSA, who closes her eyes, faking that she's asleep.)*

# SCENE 7

*A rainstorm. Heat lightning. The same barracks' common room. The entire group of women, including J.S. and* MELISSA, *sit around a kitchen table in very cramped quarters. There is a lot of smoking.* JELENA *is making a pot of Turkish coffee, which she eventually brings to the table as the scene progresses. She carries a tray of cups, which sit for some time on the tray before the women drink them. As the scene begins,* AZRA *is crying.* ZLATA *holds her hand. The other Bosnian women offer Kleenex and comfort.*

### AZRA

*(crying)*

Those bastards, they took our farms and land and cows . . .

### ZLATA

Oh, Azra, please don't get started.

#### J.S.

Does Azra upset you, Zlata?

#### ZLATA

No, Azra upsets Azra. It's what she does.

#### AZRA

I lived in my Banja Luka for seventy-two years. If I
could return to my village I would be happy to die
there. I cannot die here. I cannot lie down . . . You have
to lie down in order to die.

#### MELISSA

Where is your family now?

#### AZRA

*(begins to cry)*
I do not know.

#### NUNA

We can all tell you what happened to Azra. Each of us
knows, each one of us can tell you.

#### JELENA

Azra is horny. She's never had a man all these years.

*(MELISSA turns on her tape recorder.)*

ZLATA

Recording tears, recording refugee tears—sexy business.


NUNA

We can all tell you what happened to each of us. We all know everything.


JELENA

Except Zlata—none of us knows what happened to Zlata.


J.S.

Well, I do not know anything. Perhaps you'd like to tell me.


ZLATA

Why? Why should we want to tell you?


NUNA

They took her brother into a camp.


J.S.

I think we need to address Zlata's question. Do other women have these same concerns?

MELISSA

Azra had begun to share her story. I think she should
go on.

J.S.

No, actually, Nuna was sharing Azra's story.

NUNA

Do you have movie-star patients in New York? I read
that ninety percent of people in the movie business
have serious emotional problems. Can you tell us who
you see?

J.S.

That's confidential, Nuna.

NUNA

Do you dye your hair?

J.S.

Yes.

NUNA

Do you have a teenage daughter who pierces herself?
Does it hurt?

MELISSA

We're getting off track.

NUNA

Are you a Capricorn?

J.S.

I do not think Zlata feels safe.
(AZRA *is crying.*)

MELISSA

That's okay. Zlata doesn't have to talk. Azra . . .

AZRA

I did not leave our village. It was a perfect village. No one hardly raised their voice there except to call their dog or cow. They threatened me for months, but I would not go. I am thick, tough. I decided if they were going to kill me, they'd only kill me once. Then they broke into my house—they stole my cow . . .

MELISSA

Were you alone?

AZRA

There were just the oldies left, a village of oldies. We did not care if they killed us.

MELISSA

Did they hurt you?
(AZRA *cries more.*)

MELISSA

It's okay to cry.

ZLATA

Azra cries all the time. She does not get better. She just cries more and more. How does that help Azra? How does that help us to hear her cry?

NUNA

Why don't you drink the coffee? Is something wrong with the coffee?

J.S.

The coffee smells delicious. I quit caffeine six months ago.

#### NUNA

Americans are always quitting things. Why is that?
They spend their days quitting things.

#### MELISSA

Please, Azra was doing so well, we must let Azra tell her
story. Azra, tell us about your cow.

*(All the women groan.)*

#### SEADA

Oh look, the sun. It feels so good on my face.

*(SEADA gets up and, holding her baby tight, dances in
the sun.)*

#### SEADA

*(says into the recorder)*

Please, I want you to record that Seada feels safety on
her face.

*(SEADA goes and touches J.S.'s face and stares into her
eyes.)*

#### SEADA

It is because you came. Finally you came.

*(SEADA kisses her and giggles.)*

**JELENA**

Seada thinks she remembers you.

**MELISSA**

I think it is essential that we focus here. We need to let Azra finish her story.

**NUNA**

Yes, the patient must tell her story.

**ZLATA**

You keep using that word, Nuna—patient. Are we patients now? I, for one, am a doctor. I am a doctor and a refugee. I have not agreed to be a patient.

**NUNA**

*(very upset, blurts it out)*

Why don't you like us, Dr. J.S.? Why have you come all the way here not to be with us?

**J.S.**

*(a bit taken aback, but gaining her composure)*

What do you mean, Nuna?

*(JELENA lifts up a coffee. All the women laugh.)*

J.S.

I do not understand.


JELENA

Nuna does not understand why you don't drink coffee
with us . . .

> *(All the women pause and watch* J.S., *waiting for her*
> *next move.* J.S. *looks to* MELISSA *for help and* MELISSA
> *just watches her too. Finally,* J.S. *takes a sip of coffee. She*
> *smiles and drinks more. The other women smile.* J.S.
> *drinks the rest as the lights fade.)*

# SCENE 8

*Outside the barracks. It is early dawn.* ZLATA *is sitting on a chair. She has been weeping. She is visibly disturbed, and* J.S. *feels awkward about interrupting her privacy.* J.S. *enters. It is very quiet.*

J.S.

Hot.

ZLATA

Yes, and hot so late. Usually a breeze comes late.

J.S.

I need a breeze to sleep, the air, the sense of going somewhere.

ZLATA

Yes, the smells. The smells hang. Onion. Old cheese.
Garbage. All hanging like a bad mistake.


J.S.

These are difficult circumstances. I am not accustomed
to this.


ZLATA

You look different without your makeup.


J.S.

Yes?


ZLATA

Sad. Not so sure. Are you rich?


J.S.

What?


ZLATA

Are you wealthy?


J.S.

Why do you ask?

ZLATA

Because you are wearing a Christian Dior nightgown in a refugee camp. Because you were able to take time off from work.

J.S.

This is my work.

ZLATA

Oh, I see. We are work.

J.S.

Does it bother you that I am a therapist?

ZLATA

You never seem to answer questions.

J.S.

No, that is my work.

ZLATA

Do you make more money not answering questions?

J.S.

I am trained not to get in the way.

ZLATA

Of what?

J.S.

Of you.

ZLATA

How would you be in my way?

J.S.

By offering answers. By suggesting too much.

ZLATA

Wouldn't that just be a conversation? Don't people in America have conversations? Or do they only work?

J.S.

People pay me to listen to them.

ZLATA

People must be very lonely in America. *(pause)* I do not like the night—not anymore, not since the war. It is hard to sleep. I was rich like you before. My parents were very important people. I sleep now in the place of cows.

#### J.S.

How do you explain what's happened here? How could your neighbors, friends, suddenly behave like this?

#### ZLATA

I used to think it was the leaders, that men really made this war because of their hunger for power. But now I really believe it's in all of us—this thing, this monster, waiting to be let out. It waits there looking for a reason, a master, an invitation. If we are not aware of it, it can conquer us.

#### J.S.

Is it true you have such a monster in you, Zlata . . . ?

#### ZLATA

Oh, I have my ugliness. For example, I can't stand complainers. You know those people who are never happy, never satisfied. *(complaining voice)* It's too hot, it's too slow, but I wanted vanilla ice cream . . . What about you? What could drive you to violence?

#### J.S.

Oh, I don't know . . .

#### ZLATA

I think you do.

*(They sit awkwardly for a bit.)*

#### J.S.

Well, I can't stand people who apologize all the time. They make me crazy. I'm sorry, could you pass the salt? I'm sorry, but I seem to have forgotten my wallet.

#### ZLATA

What about people who borrow things and conveniently forget to return them? They act like you're selfish or crazy if you ask for your book back.

#### J.S.

What about the people who don't listen? I despise that. People who don't wait for you to finish a sentence, make up what you're thinking for you. They forget what you've told them because they never listened in the first place. They make me nuts.

#### ZLATA

Shoot them at once.

#### J.S.

Well, retraining camps maybe.

ZLATA

Pointless. Just shoot them.

> (*Both of them laugh at themselves. Suddenly,* J.S. *real-izes that* ZLATA *is shaking all over.*)

J.S.

What is it, Zlata?

ZLATA

Don't, don't do that psychiatrist thing with me. Has this all been a technique, a trick to get me to talk?

J.S.

What is it?

ZLATA

You only care about the story, the gory details of the story. That's all any of you want.

J.S.

I want to be your friend.

ZLATA

You don't understand that this happened to us—to real people. We were just like you, we weren't ready for this—nothing in our experience prepared us—there were no signs—we weren't fighting for centuries—it didn't come out of our perverted lifestyle—you all want it to be logical—you want us to be different than you are so you can convince yourselves it wouldn't happen there, where you are. That's why you turn us into stories, into beasts, Communists, people who live in a strange country and speak a strange language—then you can feel safe, superior. Then, afterward, we become freaks, the stories of freaks—fax, please—get us one raped Bosnian woman, preferably gang-raped, preferably English-speaking.

#### J.S.

Teach me, Zlata. Teach me how to help you.

#### ZLATA

Help. Why do you assume I want your help? You Americans don't know how to stop helping. You move so fast, cleaning things up. Fixing.

#### J.S.

I am a doctor, Zlata.

I was a doctor, too, before the war. I was the head of the pediatrics unit in Prijedor's main hospital. Now I am a refugee. Now I stare off at the stars without explanation. I look out at the beet fields and weep for no reason.

# SCENE 9

J.S. *and* MELISSA'S *room.* MELISSA *is listening to her recorder and taking notes.* SEADA *lies asleep in* J.S.'s *bed.* J.S. *enters from outside.*


J.S.

I'm having a hard time with the recorder, Melissa.

*(*J.S. *goes out.* MELISSA *puts on her headphones.* J.S. *returns, drying her face. She taps* MELISSA *on the shoulder.)*


J.S.

*(speaking loudly)*

I don't mean just now. The recorder is changing the nature of things. They're either performing for it or resisting. They need to feel safe.

*(referring to* SEADA*)*

Right. Safe.

J.S.

It feels invasive.

MELISSA

This recorder has helped women everywhere I've been. It is a device which legitimizes their experience, documents it, heals it . . .

J.S.

It's a recorder, Melissa.

MELISSA

We're here to trigger, provoke, release. Move in, move out.

J.S.

I appreciate your intensity, but . . . the way you approach things.

MELISSA

My *intensity*—you appreciate my intensity . . .

I'm sorry, it is a loaded word.

**MELISSA**

Intense, that's what they always call women who do their job, who don't apologize, or hand-hold . . . intense, extreme, hard, difficult, bitch . . .

**J.S.**

Melissa, I said I *appreciated* your intensity. In fact, I do. You're very brave. You don't waste time. You take charge. I admire that. I admire you. It's just I think sometimes you need to hang back a little. You need to watch, wait . . .

**SEADA**

*(waking up)*

Mommy . . . it's morning. It's morning, Mommy.

**MELISSA**

I'm watching, Mommy. I'm waiting.

# SCENE 10

*Laughter. Whole group of the women by the river, dangling toes in water.* AZRA, JELENA *have bright green cleansing masks on their faces.* NUNA *is smoothing on the masks like a professional skin-care person.* J.S. *watches, and* MELISSA *takes photographs, being careful to avoid photographing* ZLATA, *who reads a book.*

### NUNA

The most thoughtful refugee item yet. Sent by a French cosmetics company.

### ZLATA

Of course it's French. Who else would think of skin cleansing in the middle of ethnic cleansing?

JELENA

So much better than those canned sardines. They send them every day.

NUNA

Took me days to convince most of these women that beauty still matters. I think Azra's stopped bathing altogether.

JELENA

Have you ever noticed a sardine? It's not a fish, really. It's a thing that grows in a can. It no longer has any connection to being alive. It hardly remembers sun or sky or water. Covered in oil, in scum. It survives on the memory of all these things. It survives on the closeness to the other sardines. Sardines/refugines. Or is it surviving? Are we surviving?

ZLATA

Yes.

NUNA

No, we're waiting. Refugees wait.

MELISSA

What are you waiting for?

#### JELENA

Tomatoes. I haven't had a fresh vegetable for three months.

#### NUNA

To talk to my friends on the telephone.

#### ZLATA

Quiet. I am waiting for it to be quiet.

#### MELISSA

Maybe we could go around. I'd love to know what each of you is waiting for. We could make a kind of group poem out of it. It will allow everyone a chance to share what they're waiting for. Come on.

#### ZLATA

Maybe everyone doesn't need to *share* or want to *share*, Melissa.

#### AZRA

Well, I'm waiting to die. If someone would just bring me back to Banja Luka, I'd lie down and die with pleasure. I'd lie down with my cow.

> (NUNA *begins to put the green mask on* J.S.'s *face and* SEADA, *in a panic, runs and stops her.*)

#### SEADA

Don't do it. It will hurt her face. She doesn't need it.
She has perfect skin.

#### J.S.

Why don't I do you, Nuna? Not that you need it.

#### NUNA

People in America have facials all the time, don't they?
No one has bad skin. Everyone's beautiful and perfect.

#### J.S.

You're beautiful, Nuna.

#### JELENA

She looks like her mother.

#### NUNA

No, I look like my daddy. I am lean like him, and wiry.
I have his mouth and hands. That's how I remember
him. *(looks at her hands)* His artistic daddy hands.

#### MELISSA

Is your father alive, Nuna?

ZLATA

There she goes, story vulture.

NUNA

My father isn't dead. He's in Sarajevo. He is one of them, and so they would not let him leave.

MELISSA

But if he's your father, aren't you one of them, too?

NUNA

Those of us who are both are neither one. We are enemies everywhere.

J.S.

Not here, Nuna.

NUNA

No, not here where we have nothing—no land, no country, no things. There is nothing to kill for. But inside me it's really violent. One part of me hates the other part.

AZRA

Nuna, Nuna, hush . . . hush . . .

#### MELISSA

I think it's good for her to get it out.

#### NUNA

I used to think before the war how beautiful that all this had come together inside of me. All this history, knowledge, culture. Before the war, we who were mixed were considered the most beautiful, because so much had gone into making us. Now we are dirt—we are smudges. There was a soldier who was half-and-half like me. He slit his own mother's throat to prove to the army that he was one of them. I dream of them sucking the other half out of me with leeches. But I can never decide which part the other would be, Mommy or Daddy. You ask me what I'm waiting for—I'm waiting for someone to respect me, to see me as their own.

#### JELENA

I am waiting for booze.

#### AZRA

There is booze. Did you say there was booze?

#### MELISSA

You want to escape, Jelena, but you still haven't really answered what you're waiting for.

I want to get drunk, Melissa, happy, smashed, shit-faced, sloshed.

(*The women cheer.*)

Yes, drunk, escape . . .

You keep pushing, Melissa. You keep pushing and pushing.

That's because she's a Capricorn. They never give up.

Sometimes it's important to give up—to just surrender and let things take their course.

Sometimes it's important to just get drunk. (*reaches into a bag next to her and pulls out a bottle of booze*) Booze, booze is here.

(*The women let out a huge cheer.* MELISSA *is caught off guard. Music from Bosnia-Herzegovina plays. The women sing and dance.* J.S. *watches. She is totally moved by the singing, suspended as if caught in another time.* MELISSA *tries to participate, dances a little, but is disturbed by the drinking.* J.S. *suddenly realizes* ZLATA *is not there. She goes to find her.* MELISSA *tries to leave. The women drag her back, urging her to drink and join the fun. Music out.)*

# SCENE 11

*Stars and moonlight and crickets. We hear the women singing, and music continues in the distance.* ZLATA *sits alone.* J.S. *enters, excited and moved. She dances and moves to the music.*

### J.S.

The honesty, the rawness. The singing in one room, the women . . . oh my heart. Why didn't I just sing . . . I wanted to sing. That's all I wanted to do, was sing. Did you know I was named after Bach—yes. J. Johann S. Sebastian. Bach. J.S. Bach. I don't think he could sing.

*(They laugh.)*

### J.S.

My father. Oh boy. I was in awe of him. He was very handsome. Great musician. Perfect. It was his skill that held people. It devastated them. The obsessive, driven nature of his training. I am so goddamn well trained. I'm no different than a soldier. Marching. *(marches)* Marching. Marching through people's brains. I don't murder people, well, I do, really. I kill them with all my boundaries and rules and perfect training. You were all singing. You were just singing. Singing like friends, singing. . . . You must always know where you're going, he said, my father said, particularly in music. You must always take the song. Never let the song take you. That is why we train, practice. So we are not sloppy and sentimental.

#### ZLATA

Heaven forbid.

#### J.S.

I would never be a great singer. So I simply stopped singing.

#### ZLATA

Maybe you didn't want to be a great singer. Maybe you just wanted to sing. Why don't you sing for me?

J.S.

*(vehement)*

No, I am no longer a person who can sing. I'm trained. I'm a psychiatrist. I'm not sloppy . . . no, not me . . . *(spinning in circles until she collapses)*

*(The women's singing becomes loud, distinct, emotional, as a fantastically drunk* JELENA *leads all the women outside, a circus of singing, dancing refugees.)*

ZLATA

Sing. Come on, everybody. Sing.

*(The women surround* J.S. *and* ZLATA *and sing and dance with all their hearts.* SEADA *is truly wild, stripping away her clothes as she dances. Music out.)*

# SCENE 12

*Lights come up on* J.S. *peering into a large hole in the ground. Moans come from the hole.*

J.S.

*(worried)*

Have you hurt yourself?

AZRA

*(clearly drunk)*

No, I am dying. This is my grave.

J.S.

It is cold in there, Azra, and dirty.

AZRA

Death is like that.

J.S.

Are you sick?

AZRA

No, I told you—I am dying.

J.S.

I think it is the vodka, Azra.

AZRA

It is the war. I will close my eyes now. They will come for me soon.

J.S.

But then you never will get home, not to Bosnia.

AZRA

Bosnia is over. Bosnia is a dream.

J.S.

Isn't all of this a dream, really?

AZRA

Don't confuse me. I'm trying to die.

#### J.S.

I would miss you, Azra. I would feel terrible if you were to die here in this hole.

#### AZRA

You would get over it. Everyone gets over everything eventually. Everyone forgets.

#### J.S.

I could not forget you, Azra. Not your face, your kind, deep, welcoming face.

#### AZRA

I am ugly and old. Let me die.

#### J.S.

What would it take for you to live?

#### AZRA

I cannot remember.

#### J.S.

Sure you can, Azra. One thing. Tell me one thing that would get you to live.

AZRA

Blossom.

J.S.

What?

AZRA

My cow, Blossom. She was full the last time I saw her. She was waiting for me to milk her. I had my pail, and they forced me to leave with my empty pail, to leave Blossom.

J.S.

Can you talk to Blossom?

AZRA

From here? I don't know if she can hear me from the grave.

J.S.

I know she can hear you, Azra.

AZRA

It's too crazy.

Why don't you try it?

*(long silence)*

AZRA

*(as if calling to a cow in a field)*

Blossom! Blossom! It's me, your old friend Azra. I wanted to say good-bye, Blossom. I wanted to milk you one last time.

J.S.

What is Blossom doing?

AZRA

She's staring at me with her big brown eyes. She's just standing there, not moving.

J.S.

Is she afraid?

AZRA

Confused. She doesn't know what I'm doing in a hole. She thinks I'm playing a game with her.

J.S.

What do you want to do with her?

AZRA

I want to rub her cow skin and walk her into the fields
and watch her feed on the grass.


J.S.

But how will you do that if you are in the hole, Azra?
 (*Suddenly* AZRA *crawls out from the hole.*)


AZRA

Blossom, are you here? Where are you, Blossom?


J.S.

She is waiting for you, Azra. And she remembers you.
 (J.S. *helps* AZRA *get out of the hole.* J.S. *gradually helps
 her dust herself off and stand up.*)


AZRA

Blossom . . . Blossom . . . Blossom . . .
 (J.S. *carries a drunk and weary* AZRA *across the lawn as
 night light fades.*)

# SCENE 13

*Barracks. Morning. Lights comes up at first on* JELENA, *who has a terrible black eye.* ZLATA *makes an herbal salve for it. Everyone is hungover except* MELISSA.

JELENA

I don't mind my eye, really. It's a reminder, a badge of sorts.

NUNA

He hit you, that bastard. He hit you.

AZRA

Salami. I stick with salami.

JELENA

I was so happy last night, alive like I used to be before.

I woke Dado to dance, to dance with me. This frightened him, as he'd been drinking, and he'd passed out. But this didn't put me off. I felt light-headed and full of a kind of perfect faith, full of God. "Dado," I said last night. "Dado, you must get up and dance with me under the stars, rise up, remember." And I must have pulled at him roughly and I frightened him and he just went mad, started screaming about not taking him outside, the knives, how he'd do anything, not to hurt him, not to hurt the others—his father, that was his father and brother, to stop with the knives, stop carving his father, his fingers, his chest, his father. To stop. And he started begging, crying like a little boy, and when he found himself all little on the ground, all pathetic and groveling, he went even madder for me to see his weakness, hating that I loved him, worthless coward—and then, of course, proved that he wasn't. But I felt nothing. Nothing. Dado's fists and words, they could not touch me. I was with the old Dado. This new one, this new mutation of war, could not invade my happiness, could not invade my great dance under the stars.

MELISSA

The booze was clearly not a good idea.

JELENA

The booze made us happy for the first time in months.

MELISSA

You got beaten up. I would not be surprised if she has broken bones.

J.S.

It is my fault. I have not been thinking clearly.

MELISSA

We are not doing well here. I don't think vodka is going to be the ticket, ladies, to get you out of this refugee camp. There is no shortage of alcoholic refugees.

AZRA

Now we're alcoholics.

ZLATA

Traumatized alcoholic war victims.

NUNA

Even more spooky.

MELISSA

We need to get serious.

JELENA

Last night was the best thing that has happened to me.
I danced. I felt happy.

MELISSA

But how long can you go on like that, Jelena? You'll
have to be drunk all the time.

JELENA

What's wrong with that?

MELISSA

*(losing it)*

This is serious. Your lives are at stake. We are not looking at anything here.

J.S.

Melissa is right. Maybe the booze wasn't a great idea. It
wasn't responsible.

JELENA

What is responsible?

MELISSA

Please, we need to address what's really going on here.
We have big problems. Where is Seada?

#### NUNA

Seada was too hungover. She couldn't get up. She's really a mess.

#### MELISSA

Seada is borderline and should not be getting drunk.

#### ZLATA

Seada's doing fine.

#### NUNA

Zlata, come on. Seada is pretty screwed up.

#### ZLATA

Seada's doing fine.

#### MELISSA

Yes, because she has all of us—we support her fantasy world, we agree with her delusions. But she can't rely on us her whole life.

#### ZLATA

Why not?

MELISSA

Because she's living a lie. She's in complete denial. It's killing her.

ZLATA

No, Melissa. What happened to her during the war is killing her. Her what you call "denial" is keeping her alive.

MELISSA

Barely. She has nightmares almost every night. She's hysterical or wildly depressed most of the time.

AZRA

Who isn't?

MELISSA

Listen, there are ways to get better, to relieve the pain. It's scary to look at things. I know. But I promise it will not kill you—it's actually resisting the truth that is causing the greatest pain.

ZLATA

Again the assumptions—that we are sick and you know better than us what we need.

**MELISSA**

Zlata, you're very scared. I can feel it. You're holding the whole group back based on your own fear and anger.

**AZRA**

What is Zlata afraid of?

**NUNA**

Her story. That's why she hasn't told it to any of us.

**JELENA**

We are fighting with each other. I don't like that we are fighting.

**J.S.**

Maybe we should just slow down a little. I understand you want to get to issues, Melissa, but there is a natural human process going on here.

**MELISSA**

And what does that involve, J.S.? Drinking? Denial? Depression? Battery?

**J.S.**

Maybe. Maybe we need to be with all that for a while.

No, J.S., no. We can't wait anymore. It's too dangerous. Can you guarantee me that the next time Jelena's happy, Dado will not kill her? Can you assure me that Seada will not kill herself? We need to address some basic issues here.

J.S.

Like what?

MELISSA

Like what the hell happened to Seada. What made her like us.

ZLATA

Why do you, Melissa, need to know? That's up to Seada to tell us.

AZRA

I do not think we should talk about it behind her back. It's bad luck.

MELISSA

Azra, if we know what happened to Seada, we can help her begin to talk about it. We can prepare her for her feelings. Otherwise she will be consumed by what she refuses to remember.

#### J.S.

Zlata's right. It's Seada's story. It's up to her to tell it.

#### MELISSA

No, it's everyone's story. You have never been at war, J.S. It's a completely different dynamic. I thought that's why you wanted me here.

#### J.S.

I did. I do.

#### NUNA

Seada lived with her mother and husband.

> (MELISSA *turns her recorder on.* ZLATA *gets up to leave.*)

#### J.S.

Where are you going?

> (ZLATA *stares at everyone and storms out. The group pauses, waits.* NUNA *continues.*)

#### NUNA

Seada was wildly in love with her husband, who was very handsome. They had a beautiful life in this small village,

Donji Vackuf, and a beautiful little three-month-old baby, Doona. You could say it was paradise there. Beautiful mountains, everyone took care of everyone—even the Gypsies came there. When the soldiers came . . .

### AZRA

The soldiers came like that to all the villages. No one could believe they were coming, no one could believe they would hurt their neighbors, people thought they were just crazy kids, crazy boys, no one prepared. . . . One of the boys who beat me with a stick—I breast-fed him when he was an infant, when his mother was too sick.

### NUNA

They got the people to come from their houses. They made them come into the square. It was all casual.

(SEADA *suddenly appears in the shadows, holding her baby, overhearing the conversation.*)

### JELENA

Seada was the most beautiful girl in the village. Her husband had heard of the rapes, heard how the soldiers had been raping the young girls, so they hid Seada in the house. They did not come out into the square.

#### NUNA

The soldiers found them, though, at night. They tried to take Seada. Her mother and her husband put up a fight and they shot them just like that, both of them right there, right in the head. Seada saw this happen. She was holding her baby, her baby, Doona, and she went mad. She started running and running. She ran into the night. The soldiers couldn't stop her. They chased her, but she was running like the wind. She ran for hours without stopping.

#### AZRA

Oh, I think we should stop here. It is wrong.

#### JELENA

When you are running crazy like that, anything can happen. You can lose your way.

#### AZRA

You can lose your mind.

#### NUNA

Or . . . your baby. You can lose your baby. You can drop your baby.

J.S.

Seada dropped her baby? She dropped her little
Doona?

NUNA

She dropped her as she was running. She dropped her
in the night, along her way.

J.S.

Oh my God. Oh my God.

(SEADA *looks down at her bundle of rags and unfolds it
and screams at the top of her lungs.*)

SEADA

Doo . . . Doo . . . Doona.

(*The women scream, stand, shocked.*)

SEADA

Doona. Doona. I have to find Doona.

(SEADA *runs out. All the women move to follow her.* J.S.
*joins them.*)

JELENA

No, J.S. . . . you stay here.

J.S.

I want to come, Nuna. I want to find Seada.


JELENA

We will find her!
(*The women quickly exit in search of* SEADA.)


J.S.

(*very upset, confronting* MELISSA)
Seada heard her story. She was not prepared. This was
wrong, Melissa.


MELISSA

You need to get a hold of yourself, J.S. Your emotions
are all over the place.
(J.S. *loses it. She paces, sees the tape recorder and picks it
up. She smashes it to the ground.*)


J.S.

These women have suffered terribly and still they are
trying to trust us.


MELISSA

Don't lecture me.

We are not tape recorders. You do not get to hit and run. Seada didn't have her terrible experience in order to serve your book.

MELISSA

If people don't read Seada's story, they will never know it happened.

J.S.

This isn't about Seada. This is about you and your hunger for fame.

MELISSA

I may want recognition, but only so my work will be seen and these women, their pain, will be heard.

J.S.

And what if no one reads your book, or reads your book and doesn't care, doesn't do anything? What will all of this have meant to you—to you, Melissa?

MELISSA

This isn't about me, J.S. Everything for you is about the I . . . the big American, self-centered I. . . . You make thousands of dollars sitting in a room with it, cultivating it, expanding it.

J.S.

What happened to you that you are so numb?

MELISSA

Oh, spare me the pretending-to-be-caring analytical question.

J.S.

Okay. You're a lost little girl trying to find yourself in the middle of big, scary wars . . .

MELISSA

Maybe I am. Maybe I am. Maybe I'm familiar—too familiar with cruelty and violence—and maybe it came too early. So what? I think you're jealous. I think you would love to be me. I think you're suddenly aware that you waited too long for your life to happen and now you're lonely and old, and you don't know where to begin.

#### J.S.

*(rage exploding)*

I don't like you, Melissa. I . . .

*(NUNA breaks in, out of breath.)*


#### NUNA

Come fast. Seada is hurting herself. It's very bad.

*(NUNA grabs a very embarrassed and emotional J.S. The three of them run out. A wailing sound grows in intensity.)*

# SCENE 14

*Outside, under the stars.* SEADA *is on the ground, digging madly at the dirt, eating it, pulling her hair, rocking back and forth.* MELISSA *approaches* SEADA *right away, and* SEADA *screams, clearly believing* MELISSA *is a soldier.* MELISSA *backs off.*

SEADA

Mommy! Mommy!
>   (SEADA *frantically pulls her hair while eating dirt.* J.S., *scared, not sure what to do, watches, then suddenly grabs* SEADA *and stops her from hurting herself.* SEADA, *terribly lost, stares at her.*)

SEADA

Mommy? Mommy?
>   (SEADA *throws her arms around her neck and clings.*)

Mommy! Mommy!

(J.S. *lets her stay there for a minute. Then she gently takes her arms down and looks* SEADA *in the face.*)

J.S.

No, Seada, no Mommy. J.S. . . . I'm J.S. . . . I'm right here.

(J.S. *holds on to* SEADA.)

SEADA

No Mommy. No Mommy.

(She *starts to hurt herself again, but* J.S. *stops her.* SEADA *starts to move away, but* J.S. *grabs her and holds her back. They struggle a bit.*)

SEADA

(*wildly anxious*)

No Mommy. No Mommy.

J.S.

It's okay, Seada. I'm right here.

(SEADA *begins to punch* J.S.*'s chest.*)

SEADA

Please, I say, please, can't you help me—help me find my

baby. Believe me, I was a good mother. Happy until the war came to our village. Please, can't you help me. *(suddenly mad and panicked)* Those lights, those bright mean lights, and those voices, those loud deep voices laughing, making fun of me. *(J.S. holds her tighter, and* SEADA *connects with her again)* My aching breasts hungry to feed, overflowing with milk for Doona, as they tear off my blouse, these loud, laughing voices wearing black masks, stinking of shit and meat, tear off my milk-stained blouse and rip at my aching, full breasts, biting them, sucking, "Okay, Mommy, I'll be your little, dirty baby"—as the other one spreads my legs and the other holds my arms—Doona— "We'll show you how to make real babies, real clean babies. We'll fill you with the right kind of babies." Then he shoves himself into me, and there is a tearing, a ripping, the center of my dress, my underpants, splitting me apart, and as I'm splitting I can hear her suddenly, hear her crying out for her mother *(wails like her baby)*, Doona, crying and crying, I cannot stop it, I cannot get it out of my brain. *(tears at her hair, begins to seriously hurt herself as she continues to wail;* J.S., *terrified, grabs her and rocks her)* Mama. Mama. *(gets quiet, confessional)* Mama, I've lost my baby. I've lost our little Doona. *(puts her arms around* J.S.'s *neck and weeps like a baby; as she calms a little, the wailing still continues in her head)*

*(J.S. holds* SEADA. J.S. *weeps. She pauses.* J.S. *and* ZLATA *exchange looks. She rocks* SEADA *slowly and then, tentatively at first,* J.S. *begins to sing a nursery song. She is awkward initially, slightly out of tune, then she gathers herself, gaining her momentum and confidence in her singing.*

*As she sings to* SEADA *and the women, she finds her spirit, she breaks open, singing with heart and soul in full intensity. As she sings,* SEADA *stops crying. The wailing in her head begins to subside, then stops. The women gather round, appreciating this beautiful song, appreciating* J.S. *singing her song.*

*There is silence.)*

### MELISSA

I did not mean to hurt Seada. I did not mean to hurt anyone . . . this is my job, this is my, I am here to help . . . I am here to find a way to . . . I am here to . . .

### SEADA

Hurt. Hurt.

### MELISSA

What?

*(The other women start to laugh.)*

**NUNA**

I think she needs you to hurt.

**MELISSA**

Hurt. Hurt. Do you think I do not hurt? It's not my job to take up space here with my hurt.

(MELISSA *takes a beat, then exits. The women pause.*)

**AZRA**

At least we don't have to pretend there's a baby anymore.

# SCENE 15

*J.S. enters* MELISSA *and* J.S.*'s room in the barracks.* MELISSA *has been packing.* MELISSA *can be heard vomiting offstage.* J.S. *pauses uncomfortably.* MELISSA *comes out of the bathroom, sees* J.S., *and is embarrassed. She immediately resumes packing.*

J.S.

You're leaving?

MELISSA

I got the visa.

J.S.

Visa, to where?

MELISSA

Chechnya. I'm very excited. I'm thinking it will be the final chapter of the book.

Chechnya? You're going to Chechnya from here?

MELISSA

Yes.

J.S.

Are you eating?

MELISSA

What?

J.S.

Are you eating?

MELISSA

Don't get involved.

J.S.

We're not in America, where we get paid not to get involved, Melissa. We're here.

MELISSA

I used to have nightmares, violent nightmares all the time. I was paralyzed, then I started traveling and documenting the stories of women. And guess what? The nightmares went away.

J.S.

What do you dream about now?

MELISSA

I don't dream at all. Not my verb. I write, I do, I go.
(MELISSA *quickly finishes packing, grabs her bag, and exits.* J.S. *is left alone.*)

# SCENE 16

J.S. *sits outside under the stars, clearly disturbed. It is late.*
ZLATA *comes upon her, embarrassed.*

ZLATA

Hot.

J.S.

Yes, and hot so late.

ZLATA

Usually a breeze comes late.

J.S.

I need the breeze to sleep, the air, the sense of going
somewhere.

**ZLATA**

Yes, the smells. The smells hang. Onion. Old cheese. Garbage. All hanging like a bad mistake.

**J.S.**

Mistakes. Oh, I have learned a lot about mistakes this trip. I am the queen of mistakes.

**ZLATA**

And what would that make Melissa?

**J.S.**

Ah, Melissa . . .

**ZLATA**

Off to the Russian chapter. *(pause)* I am impressed. Really. Doctor to doctor. You did good.

**J.S.**

Really?

**ZLATA**

Really.

#### J.S.

To be honest, too many of my patients stay the same way year after year. Oh, they learn the language of therapy, they move their neurosis around, rearrange it with new psychoterminology, but their souls, their hearts, do not open. They do not change.

#### ZLATA

For refugees, things do not change. You were our change.

#### J.S.

I'm having a hard time packing. I can't seem to organize my things.

#### ZLATA

What do you think it means, Dr. Freud?

#### J.S.

I don't want to go there.

#### ZLATA

Maybe you don't want to leave us.

#### J.S.

Maybe I'm not sure why I am going back.

*(J.S. scratches herself.)*

ZLATA

Why are you scratching? What is it?

J.S.

Nothing. It's nothing.

ZLATA

Let me see.

J.S.

No, no. I'm fine.

ZLATA

Come on, open your shirt. Let me see.
(J.S. *reluctantly opens her shirt, rolls up her sleeves.*)

J.S.

I think I have measles.
(ZLATA *laughs.*)

ZLATA

It is a rare breed of Bosnian heat rash. I have a cure.

J.S.

No, no. I'm fine.

ZLATA

I'll be right back.

> (ZLATA *exits and then returns with ointment. She begins to apply it to* J.S.*'s neck and arms.*)

J.S.

Oh, it's so cool.

ZLATA

> (*as she's applying cream*)

It's for babies.

> (J.S. *begins to cry.*)

ZLATA

What is it?

J.S.

Nothing. This is not your problem.

> (J.S. *gets up to go.*)

J.S.

It's the . . .

ZLATA

. . . beauty. Bosnia. Bosnia was beautiful. The song of

Bosnia, the world of Bosnia that flows cold clean in the stream and tastes like a full meal. Bosnia, the snowy mountains, the green green hurt heart of Bosnia, the kindness we shared, how we lived in each other's warm kitchens, in sunny cafés, in the room of Bosnia. In the place, my place, my room. Gone. The ancient bridges, the mosques, the churches broken now, blown to bits and pieces. It isn't the cruelty that broke my heart. Cruelty is easy. Cruelty, like stupidity, is quick, immediate. They break in, they wear masks, they smell bad, they have machetes, they chop off the heads of my old parents sitting on their couch. There is blood, lots of it. There is screaming. There are dead, headless bodies. Cruelty is generic. Cruelty is boring, boring into the center of the part of you that goes away. We are dead— all of us—to the suffering. There is too much of it—but remind us of the beauty, the beet fields in full bloom, the redness of the fields. Remind us how we once sang, how the voices echoed as one through the landscape of night and stars. Remind us how often we laughed, how safe we felt, how easy it was to be friends. All of us. I miss everything—Bosnia was paradise.

(J.S. *and* ZLATA *look at each other and lights fade.*)

# SCENE 17

J.S., *in her New York apartment, talking into a recorder.*

### J.S.

Okay, Melissa. I'm here. I'm talking into a tape recorder. Can you believe it? Hello, hello. Helloooo, Melissa. I'd sing, but I'm not drunk. I still need to be a little. drunk to sing. God knows where you are now . . . Chechnya, Kosovo . . .

What if I told you that Zlata stopped my life, made my luxurious, advantaged, safe, protected, well-kept, organized, professional life impossible? What if she entered me, and I could not move? Back. Could not return to anything, anyone I'd ever been.

I have amnesia. I am no longer hungry. I am empty. I have lost my desire. America makes no sense to me. I am after nothing. What if this woman, Zlata, her

heart, were to bleed into mine and I were to hemor-
rhage, and we were to bleed together? Would you say
I'd lost all boundaries, that I was no longer professional, or would you say BLEED, BLEED?

(*The women at the refugee camp gather around the
kitchen table in Bosnia to make coffee.*)

And then, what if I were to tell you that I was not unhappy? No, my ambition, my need to achieve, have it,
have more, was the thing that made me unhappy. Always unhappy, always longing for more. Longing to be
someone, to count, to matter, to make it. That was my
unhappiness. I am without a country. I am without a
profession or pursuit. I am without a reason or even a
direction. I am there in that refugee camp in the middle
of nowhere. I am with Zlata and Jelena and Seada and
Nuna and Azra, sometime very early in the morning.
We are sitting and we are trying, we are really trying to
trust one another, and in between the tears we take little sips of mad, thick coffee.

(J.S. *looks to the women. Lights fade.*)

## The End

# ACKNOWLEDGMENTS

First I want to thank Lauren Lloyd for finding the funds to send me to the former Yugoslavia. Then I want to thank the women who helped me so much when I got there and allowed me to enter their world: Rachael Warcham; Nela Pamukovic and the Center for Women War Victims in Zagreb; Nuna Zvizdic and Zene zenama Sarajevo (Women to Women Sarajevo); Biba Metikos; Lejla Zvizdic; Adisa Krupalija; and Rada Boric, who was from the beginning a great friend and sister, and fundamental to the project. Thanks deeply to all the brave and generous Bosnians who told me their stories.

I want to thank the Public Theater for commissioning this piece, and particularly Morgan Jenness and Shelby Jiggetts-Tivony for their early support and faith. I want to thank David Phillips for bringing it into its first public life and continuing to support it thereafter. I want to thank various institutions for allowing me to develop the play over five years: the Helen Hayes Theater, the Kennedy Center, Hartford Stage, New York Stage and Film, the Roundabout, and the Westside Arts.

I want to thank all the actors who have performed in the many readings of this play throughout its development. Bless you for your time and talents and generous spirit.

I want to thank the prime minister of Bosnia, Haris Silajdzic, and the minister of culture, Amila Kapetanovic, for their support of the play in Sarajevo.

Thank you to Pat Mitchell for jumping on a plane within twenty-four hours and coming to Sarajevo, and then for her great advocacy; and to Beth Dozoretz for her ongoing support and for producing the great reading at the Kennedy Center.

I want to thank Mollie Doyle for originally believing this play should be published, and Joy de Menil, who has been an enormously helpful editor.

Thank you to the following directors, for their dramaturgical work on the play and their great insights: Michael Mayer, Lenka Udovicki, Elinor Renfield, and, finally, Michael Wilson, for bringing *Necessary Targets* into the world as a fully produced play. I am indebted to him for his wisdom, huge heart, and great talent.

I want to thank Anita Waxman and Elizabeth Williams.

I want to particularly thank Sally Fisher, for her prodding and faith, and David Stone, for all the invisible ways he's supported this play.

Thank you to George Lane for getting behind *Necessary Targets* at the crucial moment; Charlotte Sheedy for her fierce mother-lion-like ways; and Nancy Rose, for her great protection and love.

I want to thank my friends Paula Allen and Brenda Currin, who have kept believing in me and in *Necessary Targets*.

I want to thank James Lecesne—my spiritual brother and artistic ally. Bless you for your deep wisdom and great *ichinen*.

I want to thank Gary Sunshine, for his guidance, dramaturgical wisdom, typing, faith, and loyalty. I simply could not manage without him.

I want to thank Harriet Leve for being such a steady, loving, fierce producer.

Thank you to Willa Shalit, who has singly stood by me and this play for years, with all her heart, spirit, and vision, and is responsible for ushering it into the world.

Finally, I want to thank Ariel Orr Jordan—what to say . . . his belief in me has fueled me and pushed me and opened me. I am forever grateful.

*Nam-my-o-ho-renge-kyo.*

## ABOUT THE AUTHOR

EVE ENSLER is an internationally acclaimed playwright whose many works for stage include *Floating Rhonda and the Glue Man, Lemonade, The Vagina Monologues* (for which she received an Obie Award), and *The Good Body*. Performances of *The Vagina Monologues*, sponsored by V-Day (www.vday.org), have raised over $25 million to stop violence against abused women and girls around the world. She lives in New York City.